SCHOLASTIC

WRITING PRACTICE

New York • Toronto • London • Auckland • Sydney
Mexico City • New Delhi • Hong Kong • Buenos Aires

Teaching *Resources*

Cover design by Jay Namerow
Interior illustrations by Sherry Neidigh
Interior design by Quack & Company

ISBN 0-439-81910-5

3 4 5 6 7 8 9 10   40   13 12 11 10 09 08

Table of Contents

Dear Parent:

Welcome to *1st Grade Writing Practice!* This valuable tool is designed to help your child succeed in school. Scholastic, the most trusted name in learning, has been creating quality educational materials for school and home for nearly a century. And this resource is no exception.

Inside this book, you'll find colorful and engaging activity pages that will give your child the practice he or she needs to master essential skills, such as capitalizing and punctuating statements, understanding parts of sentences, writing descriptive sentences, and so much more.

To support your child's learning experience at home, try these helpful tips:

- Provide a comfortable, well-lit place to work, making sure your child has all the supplies he or she needs.

- Encourage your child to work at his or her own pace. Children learn at different rates and will naturally develop skills in their own time.

- Praise your child's efforts. If your child makes a mistake, offer words of encouragement and positive help.

- Display your child's work and celebrate his successes with family and friends.

We hope you and your child will enjoy working together to complete this workbook.

Happy learning!
The Editors

That's Amazing!

 *A sentence begins with a **capital letter**.*

Help the mouse through the maze by coloring each box with a word that begins with a capital letter.

The	For	That	with	know	but
here	on	When	Have	next	we
as	after	good	Make	there	see
Go	Look	Are	Could	is	why
This	who	said	in	come	them
Has	Name	Before	Her	Where	The

 Read the back of a cereal box. How many capital letters did you find? Write the number next to the cheese.

Squeak!

Circle the words that show the correct way to begin each sentence.

1. The mouse
   the mouse
   is looking for food.

2. he finds
   He finds
   a cracker on the floor.

3. he Eats
   He eats
   the cracker.

4. Then he
   then He
   takes a nap.

5. oh No,
   Oh no,
   he hears a cat!

6. the Mouse
   The mouse
   runs home fast!

Counting Sheep

Write the beginning words correctly to make a sentence.

1. we read _____ books before bed.

2. then we _____ hug good night.

3. my bed _____ is soft and cozy.

4. my cat _____ sleeps with me.

5. the sky _____ has turned dark.

6. my eyes _____ close.

On another piece of paper, copy a sentence from your favorite bedtime book.
Circle the capital letter at the beginning.

Scholastic Teaching Resources

Sweet Dreams!

Write each beginning word correctly to make a sentence.

1. my dog

_____

_____   runs in her sleep.

2. she must

_____

_____   be dreaming.

3. maybe she

_____

_____   is chasing a cat.

4. sometimes she

_____

_____   even barks.

5. i think

_____

_____   it is funny.

 On another piece of paper, write a sentence about a dream you remember. Circle the capital letter at the beginning.

The Night Sky

*A **telling sentence** ends with a **period**.*

period

Add a period to each sentence.

1. Many things shine in the sky at night____

2. The moon looks the brightest____

3. It is closest to Earth____

4. The stars look like tiny dots____

5. They are very far away____

6. The sun is a star____

7. Planets look like colored stars____

8. Their light does not twinkle____

9. Shooting stars look like stars that are falling____

10. There are many things to see in the night sky____

Twinkle, Twinkle Little Star

Rewrite each sentence using periods.

1. Tonight I saw a star

_____

_____

2. I saw the star twinkle

_____

_____

3. It looked like a candle

_____

_____

4. It was very bright

_____

_____

5. I made a wish

_____

_____

6. I hope it comes true

_____

_____

 Look for the brightest star in the sky. Make a wish. On another piece of paper, write a sentence about your wish.

Hop to It!

 *A **telling sentence** begins with a **capital letter** and ends with a **period**.*

Rewrite each sentence correctly.

1. frogs and toads lay eggs

2. the eggs are in the water

3. tadpoles hatch from the eggs

4. the tadpoles grow legs

5. the tadpoles lose their tails

Scholastic Teaching Resources

Hop to It Some More!

Rewrite each sentence correctly.

1. tadpoles become frogs or toads

_____

_____

2. frogs live near water

_____

_____

3. toads live under bushes

_____

_____

4. frogs have wet skin

_____

_____

5. toads have bumpy skin

_____

_____

On another piece of paper, write three sentences about a time that you saw a frog or toad. Make sure you use capital letters and periods correctly.

Patriotic Sentences

 *A **sentence** tells a complete idea. It should always make sense.*

Color the flag to show:

RED = sentence   WHITE = not a sentence

	This is a flag.
	The flag
	The flag has stars.
	The stars
	The stars are white.
	The stripes
	The stripes are red.

And white

The stripes are white.

Blue part

The flag has a blue part.

There are

There are 50 stars.

 On another piece of paper, write a complete sentence about your colorful flag.

High-Flying Sentences

Color each flag that tells a complete thought. Leave the other flags blank.

We made a flag.

The big flag

The flag is big.

Blue and purple

It is purple and blue.

I hung it in my room.

In my room

On another piece of paper, turn this into a sentence: The biggest flag.

At the Seashore

Unscramble the words to make a sentence. Write the new sentence below each picture. Finish each picture to match the sentence.

sailing are boats Five

four have We buckets

In the Rain Forest

Unscramble the words to make a sentence. Write the new sentence. Do not forget to put a period at the end.

A hiding jaguar is

blue Some butterflies are

water in jump the Frogs

snakes trees Green hang from

very tall grow The trees

 Scramble a sentence for someone at home. Be sure the first word begins with a capital letter.

Snakes Alive!

 *A sentence has a **naming part**. It tells who or what the sentence is about.*

Color the snake that tells the naming part in each sentence below.

1. The phone — is ringing.

2. My dad — is the coach.

3. Jon's hamster — ran away.

4. Our bus — was late.

5. The teacher — left his home.

6. Greg and Pete — visit us.

On another piece of paper, write one of the sentences using a different naming part.

Scholastic Teaching Resources

Slithering Sentences

Circle the naming part in each sentence below.
Then color the picture to match.

1. The blue snake is playing with a friend.

2. The yellow snake is climbing a tree.

3. The green snake hides under rocks.

4. The brown snake is swimming.

5. The red snake is hanging on a tree.

6. The purple snake sleeps in trees.

7. The black snake rests on a rock.

8. The orange snake is near an egg.

 Look around you. On another piece of paper, write three people or things that could be the naming part of a sentence.

Who Is That?

The naming part of a sentence can be a person.

Use the pictures to find naming parts to make each sentence complete.

1. _____ fell on the ice.

2. _____ won the race.

3. _____ went inside the dark cave.

4. _____ climbed the hill.

5. _____ swam across the pool.

Where Is That?

 The naming part of a sentence can be a place or a thing.

Use naming parts to complete each sentence that tells about the map.

1. _____ is near the swings.

2. _____ is far from the cave.

3. _____ is a good place to fish.

4. _____ has bats inside.

5. _____ is along Tree Lane.

 Find the naming part of three sentences in your favorite book.

Family Photos

The naming part of a sentence can be a person, a place, or a thing.

Use your own naming parts to write a complete sentence about each picture.

_____

- -

_____

_____

- -

_____

No Bones About It!

  *A sentence has an **action part**. It tells what is happening.*

Color the bone that tells the action part in each sentence below.

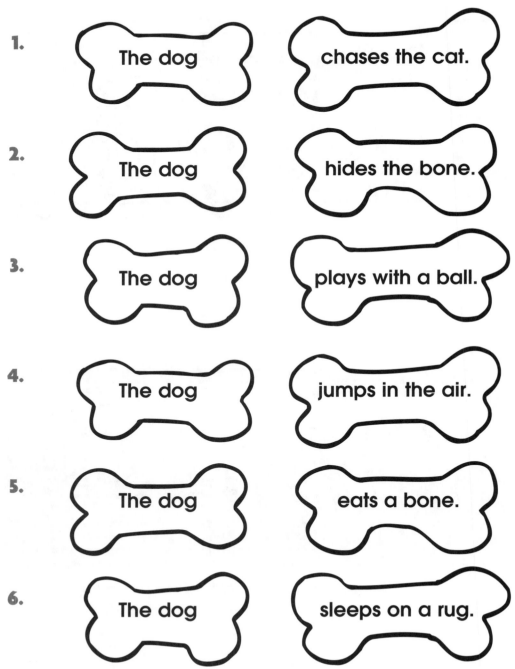

1. The dog   chases the cat.

2. The dog   hides the bone.

3. The dog   plays with a ball.

4. The dog   jumps in the air.

5. The dog   eats a bone.

6. The dog   sleeps on a rug.

 On another piece of paper, rewrite your favorite sentence.

Mighty Good Sentences

Choose the ending that tells what each dog is doing. Remember to use periods.

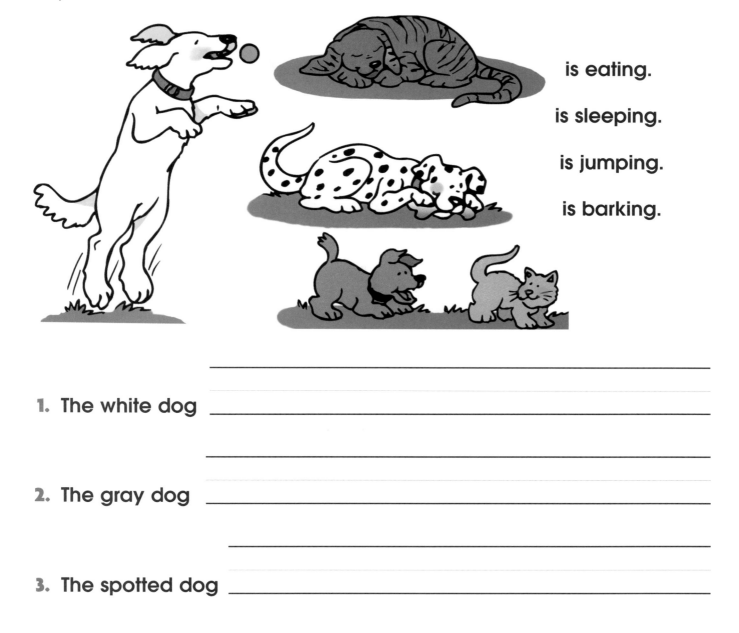

is eating.

is sleeping.

is jumping.

is barking.

1. The white dog _____

2. The gray dog _____

3. The spotted dog _____

4. The striped dog _____

On another piece of paper, draw another dog and write a sentence about it.

Scholastic Teaching Resources

A Busy Classroom

 The action part of a sentence is called the **verb**.

Complete each sentence with an action verb to tell what is happening in the picture. Remember to use periods.

1. **Mr. Downs** _____

2. **The fish** _____

3. **James** _____

4. **Cara** _____

 On another piece of paper, write a sentence about your teacher. Circle the action word.

Pencil It In

 Sometimes the verb does not show action.
It still tells what is happening.

For example: I *the answer.*

I *hungry.*

Word Bank

seems   am   gets
were   is   are
was

Choose a verb from the Word Bank
to complete each sentence.

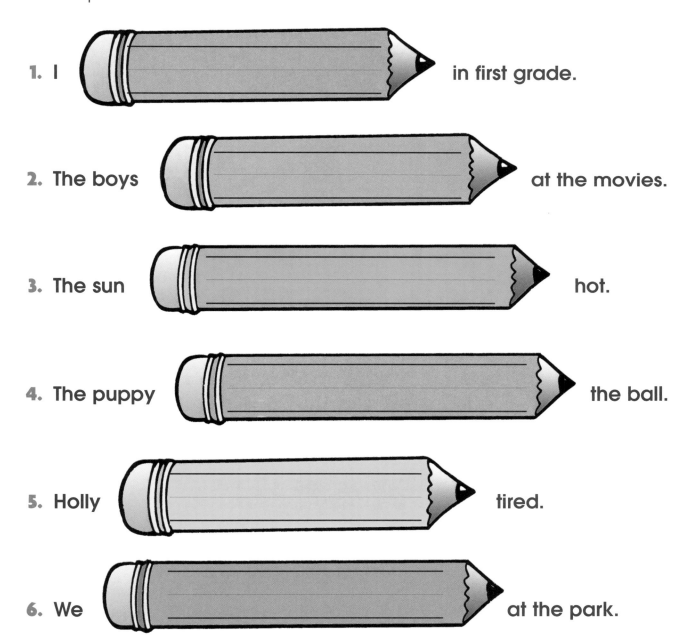

1. I _____ in first grade.

2. The boys _____ at the movies.

3. The sun _____ hot.

4. The puppy _____ the ball.

5. Holly _____ tired.

6. We _____ at the park.

Topsy-Turvy!

 A sentence has a verb that tells what is happening.

Write five silly sentences that tell what is happening in the pictures.

1. _____

_____

2. _____

_____

3. _____

_____

4. _____

_____

5. _____

The Caboose

 *A sentence is more interesting when it tells **where** the action is happening.*

In each caboose, draw a picture to show where each sentence takes place.

1.

The plane flew into the clouds.

2.

The princess played in the castle.

3.

The boys fished in the lake.

Chugging Along

Write an ending for each sentence that tells where the action takes place.

naming part   the action   where

1. The monkey   swings

2. The ball   flew

3. Jenna's family   went

4. The pig   slept

5. The glass   fell

When Was That?

 *A sentence may also tell **when** the action takes place.*

Circle the part that tells when in each sentence.

1. George Washington lived long ago.

2. The mail carrier was late yesterday.

3. The bear slept in winter.

4. We are going to the zoo today.

5. The leaves change in the fall.

6. I lost my tooth last night.

7. It rained all day.

8. The party starts at noon.

9. We got home yesterday.

10. We ate turkey on Thanksgiving Day.

11. The kitten was playing this morning.

12. Tomorrow I am going to my grandmother's house.

 On another piece of paper, make a time line of your life. Use it to write two sentences that tell when.

My Busy Day

 *Part of a sentence may tell **when** the action happened.*

Write the beginning part of each sentence to tell about your day.
Draw a picture to match each sentence.

this morning.

this afternoon.

tonight.

 On another piece of paper, write four sentences and draw four pictures to tell about your best day ever.

Silly Sentences

A sentence may have three parts: a naming part, an action, and a part that tells where or when.

Complete each missing part to make silly sentences.

the naming part	the action	where or when
1. The monkey		on his head.
2. My dad	is hopping	
3.	flipped	in the forest.
4. The ball	bounced	
5. My shoes		at the pool.
6. The snake	twisted	
7. The bubbles	filled	

 On another piece of paper, write a new sentence by scrambling three parts listed above. For example, use the naming part from #1, the action part from #2, and where or when from #3. Draw a picture of your sentence.

Sweet Sentences

Use choices from each part to make three "sweet" sentences.

naming part	action	where or when
I	ate doughnuts	at the bakery
She	ate candy	at the party
He	chewed gum	at the circus

 On another piece of paper, name the three parts of this sentence: The doughnut shop closed at noon.

Home Sweet Home

Write three sentences about the picture. For example: The dog is sleeping outside.

1. _____

_____

_____

2. _____

_____

_____

3. _____

_____

_____

The Construction Crew

Write three sentences about the picture. Include three parts in each sentence.

1. _____

2. _____

3. _____

Mystery Boxes

 Describing words help you imagine how something looks, feels, smells, sounds, or tastes.

Read the describing words to guess the mystery object. Use the Word Bank to help you.

Word Bank

bat   ball   cracker   kitten

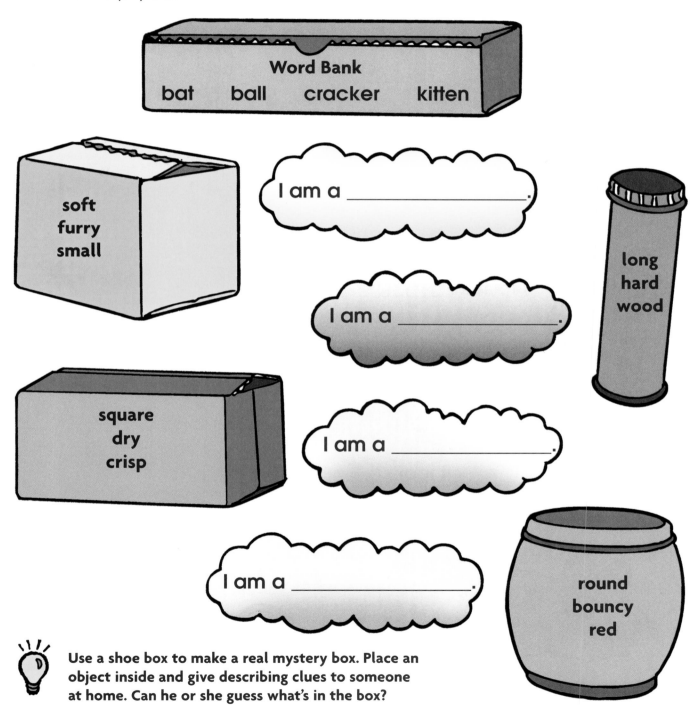

**soft
furry
small**

I am a _____.

I am a _____.

**long
hard
wood**

**square
dry
crisp**

I am a _____.

I am a _____.

**round
bouncy
red**

Use a shoe box to make a real mystery box. Place an object inside and give describing clues to someone at home. Can he or she guess what's in the box?

Sensational Words

Choose words from the Word Bank to describe each picture.

It tastes _____.

It looks _____.

It feels _____.

Word Bank

bumpy

crunchy

furry

gray

red

salty

smooth

squeaky

sweet

It feels _____.

It tastes _____.

It sounds _____.

It looks _____.

It sounds _____.

It feels _____.

 Find two objects outside. On another piece of paper, write two adjectives to describe each object.

Pretty Packages

The describing words in a sentence help the reader paint a picture in his or her mind.

Write three words to describe each gift. Then color them to match.

_____ (color)

_____ (color)

_____ (pattern)

_____ (color)

_____ (color)

_____ (pattern)

_____ (color)

_____ (color)

_____ (pattern)

_____ (color)

_____ (color)

_____ (pattern)

Describe a "mystery object" to a friend. Can he or she guess what you are describing?

What's Inside?

Use the describing words from page 37 to write a sentence about each package. For example: I found a swimsuit in the **yellow square** box.

1. I found _____ in the

_____

_____ package.

2. I found _____ in the

_____

_____ package.

3. I found _____ in the

_____

_____ package.

4. I found _____ in the

_____

_____ package.

A Walk in the Park

➡️ *Describing words make a sentence more interesting.*

Write describing words to finish each sentence.

1. A _____ duck is

   _____

   swimming in the _____ pond.

2. A _____ man is walking

   _____

   his _____ dog.

3. A _____ girl is

   _____

   flying a _____ kite.

4. A _____ woman is sitting

   _____

   on a _____ bench.

 **On another piece of paper, draw a picture of your favorite animal at the zoo.
Then write two words to describe this animal.**

Around Town

Write a sentence for each picture. Use the describing word in the sentence.

large

_____
_____
_____
_____
_____

beautiful

_____
_____
_____
_____
_____

crowded

_____
_____
_____
_____
_____

noisy

_____
_____
_____
_____
_____

 On another piece of paper, write five words that describe your street.

Keep It in Order

Sentences can be written in a particular order to tell a story.

Finish each story by writing sentences about the last pictures.

1. First, the spider crawls up.

Next, _____

Last, _____

2. First, there is a tadpole.

Next, _____

Last, _____

What's Next?

 Sentences can be written in order to give directions.

Finish each set of directions by writing sentences about the last pictures.

1. **First,** mix all the ingredients.

Next, _____

_____

Last, _____

2. **First,** put your dog in the tub.

Next, _____

_____

Last, _____

Which Title Fits?

*The name of a story is called the **title**. It matches with the story. Most of the words in a title begin with capital letters.*

Match each title with its story. Write the title above the picture.

A Big Beak	**The Big Win**
My Space Friend	**A Knight's Tale**

_____
(title)

_____
(title)

_____
(title)

_____
(title)

A Terrific Title

Fill in the missing words to make your own story. Then write a title that fits with your story. Draw a picture about your story in the box.

_____

(title)

One _____ day,

_____ took his pet

_____ for a walk. First,

they went to the _____.

Then they walked to _____'s

house. Last, they went home to _____

_____. It was a

_____ day!

Story Strips

 A story has a beginning, middle, and end.

Write a sentence to tell about each part of the story. Remember to give the story a title.

Beginning

_____
(title)

- -

Middle

- -

End

- -

More Story Strips

 A story has a beginning, middle, and end.

Think of a story you know well. Write about the beginning, middle, and end parts. Draw pictures to match. Be sure to give your story a title.

_____

(title)

Beginning

_____

Middle

_____

End

_____

 Fold a piece of paper two times to make a storybook. Write a story and draw pictures to match. Do not forget to write a title for your story.

Answer Key

Page 5

The	For	That	with	know	but
here	on	When	Have	next	we
as	after	good	Make	there	see
Go	Look	Are	Could	is	why
This	who	said	in	come	them
Has	Name	Before	Her	Where	The

Page 6
1. The mouse; 2. He finds;
3. He eats; 4. Then he; 5. Oh no,;
6. The mouse

Page 7
1. We read; 2. Then we; 3. My bed;
4. My cat; 5. The sky; 6. My eyes

Page 8
1. My dog; 2. She must; 3. Maybe she; 4. Sometimes she; 5. I think

Page 9
Check that the child has added a period to the end of each sentence.

Page 10
Check that the child has added a period to the end of each sentence.

Page 11
1. Frogs and toads lay eggs. 2. The eggs are in the water. 3. Tadpoles hatch from the eggs. 4. The tadpoles grow legs. 5. The tadpoles lose their tails.

Page 12
1. Tadpoles become frogs or toads. 2. Frogs live near water. 3. Toads live under bushes. 4. Frogs have wet skin. 5. Toads have bumpy skin.

Page 13
The following sentences should be colored red: This is a flag. The flag has stars. The stars are white. The stripes are red. The stripes are white. The flag has a blue part. There are 50 stars. The rest are not sentences and should be colored white.

Page 14

Page 15
Five boats are sailing.
We have four buckets.

Page 16
A jaguar is hiding. Some butterflies are blue. Frogs jump in the water. Green snakes hang from trees. The trees grow very tall.

Page 17
The snakes on the left side of the page should have been colored.

Page 18
1. The blue snake; 2. The yellow snake; 3. The green snake; 4. The brown snake; 5. The red snake;
6. The purple snake; 7. The black snake; 8. The orange snake

Page 19
Sentences will vary.

Page 20
Sentences will vary.

Page 21
Sentences will vary.

Page 22
The bones on the right side of the page should have been colored.

Page 23
1. is jumping. 2. is barking.
3. is eating. 4. is sleeping.

Page 24
Sentences will vary.

Page 25
1. am; 2. are or were; 3. is; 4. gets;
5. is or was or seems; 6. were or are

Page 26
Sentences will vary.

Page 27
Pictures will vary.

Page 28
Answers will vary.

Page 29
1. long ago; 2. yesterday; 3. in winter;
4. today; 5. in the fall; 6. last night;
7. all day; 8. at noon; 9. yesterday;
10. on Thanksgiving Day;
11. this morning; 12. Tomorrow

Page 30
Sentences will vary.

Page 31
Answers will vary.

Page 32
Sentences will vary.

Page 33
Sentences will vary.

Page 34
Sentences will vary.

Page 35
kitten, bat, cracker, ball

Page 36
sweet, red, smooth; bumpy, salty,
crunchy; gray, squeaky, furry

Page 37
Adjectives will vary.

Page 38
Sentences will vary.

Page 39
Sentences will vary.

Page 40
Sentences will vary.

Page 41
Sentences will vary.

Page 42
Sentences will vary.

Page 43
My Space Friend; A Big Beak;
The Big Win; A Knight's Tale

Page 44
Stories will vary.

Page 45
Sentences will vary.

Page 46
Sentences and pictures will vary.